3-D THRILLERS!

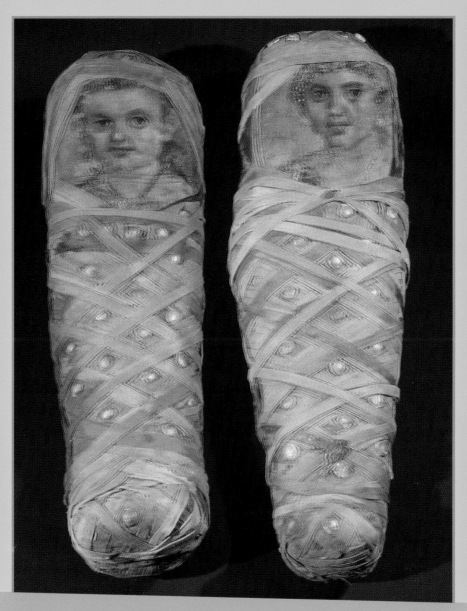

MUMMIES

DUTTON CHILDREN'S BOOKS
NEW YORK

The faces of these mummified children are covered by portrait masks. Both mummies were found in the Egyptian pyramid of Hawara and date to about A.D. 50.

Meet The Mummies

Even though mummies are found all over the world, they are actually very rare. People die all the time, but not every dead body gets preserved—far from it! Normally, when a person dies, bacteria on the body cause it to decompose, eventually leaving behind just the skeleton. But sometimes, when conditions are just right and the bacteria can be stopped, the fleshy parts of the body are preserved—and a mummy is born! Some scientists only use the word "mummy" to describe remains that have been deliberately kept from decaying, but bodies preserved naturally are often called mummies, too.

ANCIENT ANIMALS

Mummies aren't limited to people! Ancient Egyptians intentionally mummified cats, dogs, birds, crocodiles, and monkeys. And animals that die in areas where the climate is always cold are excellent candidates for accidental mummification. Prehistoric woolly mammoths that are tens of thousands of years old have been found wonderfully preserved in ice.

MUMMY MIA!

From 1599 to 1920, Sicilian monks in the Italian city of Palermo were making mummies. The earlier Sicilian mummies were preserved by drying the bodies over clay pipes for a year, but the later and better preserved ones were created by using chemicals including arsenic and milk of magnesia. Six thousand of these mummies are on display in the catacombs of a church in Palermo, Sicily.

The Guanche people, an ancient culture from the Canary Islands off the coast of Africa, also preserved their dead intentionally. The embalmers removed the internal organs, laid the body out in the sun to dry, and then stuffed it with sand. Few Guanche mummies still exist because most were ground up for medicine in the 1500s.

THE MUMMY'S CURSE?

After Howard Carter opened the tomb of the Pharaoh Tutankhamen in 1922, a series of strange things happened. First, Carter's pet canary was eaten by a cobra—the symbol of a Pharaoh's power. Then his boss, Lord Carnarvon, died suddenly. At the exact moment of his death, all the lights went out in Cairo and his dog supposedly dropped dead! Reporters falsely claimed that there was an inscription in the tomb: "Death shall come on swift wings to him that toucheth the tomb of Pharaoh." This led many people to believe that an ancient curse was to blame, but the events were probably rumors or coincidences.

BURIAL UNFIT FOR A KING

When Egyptian mummies are mentioned, we think of fancy gold coffins, the impressive tombs of the great Pharaohs, and yards of linen bandages (one mummy discovered in 1908 took an hour and a half to unwrap!). Yet the first mummies of Egypt were not given these special treatments—in fact, they weren't even purposefully preserved. Dead bodies were simply buried in shallow graves in the desert. The hot dry sand naturally dried them out and created the first Egyptian mummies.

The Mummies of

W hen the Egyptians realized that bodies buried in the hot desert sands were naturally preserved, they were pleased and took it as a sign that the souls of their relatives were living in an afterlife. They began to believe that in order to stay in the afterlife, the soul must have a mummy. But a shallow hole in the desert wasn't regal enough for the Pharaohs. They wanted huge tombs, deep underground. The sand mummies inspired them to perfect a method of artificial mummification that would enable the bodies of their dead to stick around forever!

GREAT NOSE JOB

The wonderfully preserved mummy of Ramses the Great is an example of the amazing skill of the Egyptian embalmers. Examination with X rays revealed that the mummy makers carefully stuffed Ramses' nose with peppercorns to help maintain its dignified hooked shape.

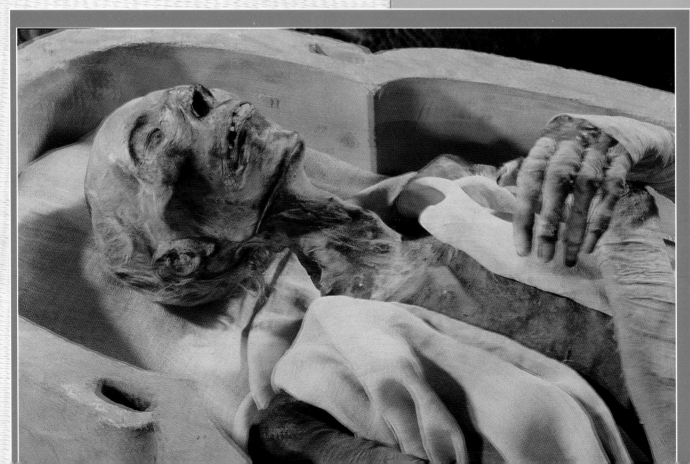

Egypt

SPECIAL STORAGE

Egyptian embalmers realized that decomposition began inside the body cavity, where all the moist organs are found. So they removed the stomach, intestines, liver, and lungs and dried them in a salty substance called natron. Each organ was stored in its own container, called a canopic jar. Since the embalmers thought the heart, not the brain, was the center of thoughts, emotions, and personality, they left it in the chest, and pulled the brain out through the nostrils.

A mummy spent its eternal afterlife in its tomb, so it needed to be prepared: food, clothes, and weapons were left for the soul to use. Early Pharaohs were buried inside pyramids, but later they were put in secret tombs deep within the Valley of the Kings near the banks of the Nile River.

LAYERS OF PROTECTION

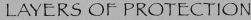

For about 40 days, a dead Pharaoh (or other Egyptian of high status) lay covered with natron to completely dry the body. Once dried, the mummy was wrapped from head to toe in layers of linen bandages. Next, a funeral mask that looked like the face of the dead person was fitted over the head. Finally, the mummy was ready to be placed into one or more coffins. Like the funeral mask, these coffins were often decorated to resemble the person inside. These portraits were intended to help the soul identify the mummy as its own!

RECENT DISCOVERY

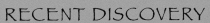

The greatest archaeological discovery of the last several years was made by . . . a donkey! While walking along a dusty road in Egypt in 1996, the donkey got its leg stuck in a small hole, which was actually a crack in the ceiling of an underground tomb. Egyptologists are especially excited by this find because the tomb is in perfect condition—it has never been looted by tomb robbers. Also, it's believed to be just one small part of an entire cemetery. There may be as many as 10,000 more mummies buried nearby!

I f you've ever seen a real mummy in a museum, it probably came from Egypt. Although Egyptian mummies are the most famous, did you know that the Egyptians were not the first people to experiment with mummification? Half a world away, in the area that is now the border between Chile and Peru, the Chinchorro people began preserving their dead two thousand years before the Egyptians! The continent of South America is home to many different types of mummies. Some were created on purpose; others were preserved accidentally by extreme weather conditions.

BASKET CASES

The Atacama Desert in Chile and Peru is home to many naturally desiccated (dried) mummies. About 1,200 years ago, Atacamian people put their dead in rope baskets and buried them in the desert. The heat and dryness of the desert preserved the bodies perfectly. Although the baskets often rotted away, the hair of many of the mummies remained intact!

Momias!

In times of drought, famine or epidemic, the Incas would sacrifice a child as a gift to the gods. Holy men took the child to the peak of an Andean mountain. They killed the child and buried the body with pottery, shells, and small figurines of animals. Five hundred years later, these bodies are still preserved due to the freezing, dry air of the mountaintops.

PRESERVED PERUVIANS

Numerous ancient cultures once lived in what is now known as Peru. These early people often tied up their dead in a crouched position, and then wrapped them in thick layers of beautifully embroidered cloth, specially crafted for burial. Some of these cultures even added fake heads to the tops of their bundled-up mummies! These false heads were often constructed out of leaf-stuffed cotton, with facial features made from shells, pieces of metal, or plant fibers.

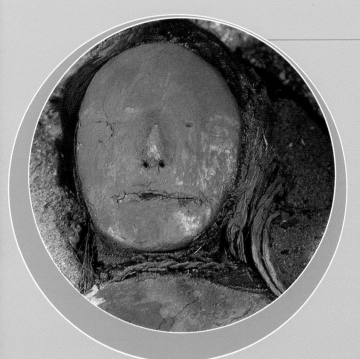

SOME ASSEMBLY REQUIRED

While digging ditches to lay new water pipes, workers in Arica, Chile, made a shocking discovery. Under just a few inches of sand lay an ancient Chinchorro cemetery of ninety-six mummies! At different times in their history, the Chinchorros used different methods to prepare their mummies. The earliest ones were made by using a sharpened pelican beak, stone, or shell to cut the body apart, remove the organs, scrape the flesh from the bones, and peel off the skin. Sticks and reeds were tied to the bones to reassemble the skeleton, and the organs and muscles were re-created by stuffing the body with clay and bundles of plant fibers. After rewrapping the body with its own skin, the mummy was painted and a clay mask was placed over its face.

Pickled People

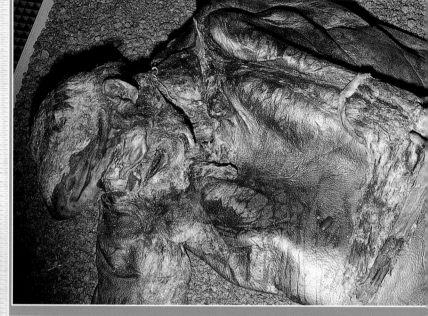

J ust as cucumbers can be preserved in liquid by pickling, human bodies are sometimes kept from decaying by the special conditions found in the water of a peat-moss bog. Lack of oxygen in the water and plenty of tannic acid work together to kill the bacteria that would otherwise make a dead body rot away. Throughout northern Europe, hundreds of bog bodies have been found, and the preserved remains show that many of these people died violent deaths—they were killed and sacrificed in brutal fashion to appease the Iron Age gods. By studying these bodies, scientists can learn a lot about ancient religions and traditions.

RECONSTRUCTING LINDOW MAN

While cutting peat in Lindow Moss, England, in 1984, workers came upon a bog body that was in bad shape. It had been damaged by the peat-cutting machine and was crushed by 2,300 years underneath thick layers of peat. Yet despite this damage and the injuries that killed him—slit throat, smashed skull, and strangulation with a knotted cord—we are still able to get a good idea of what Lindow Man looked like. Forensic scientists determined that he was between 25 and 30 years old when he died, had brown hair and a beard, and was in good health.

LAST MEAL

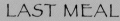

Bog bodies are usually so well preserved that scientists can determine what they ate last by examining the contents of their stomachs. The stomach of this ancient man, found near Grauballe, Denmark, in 1952, contained vegetable soup—made up of sixty-three different types of grains and plants!

# of Europe

REST IN PEACE

Tollund Man, named for the location of the Danish bog in which he was discovered in 1950, was between 30 and 40 years of age at the time of his death by hanging. Tollund Man is famous for the expression on his face—he appears to be sleeping peacefully. Archaeologists believe that his eyes and mouth were respectfully closed by his killers after he was hung as a sacrifice to the gods.

Most bog bodies have been dead between 1,500 and 2,400 years, but they are usually so well preserved that they are often mistaken as victims of recent murders!

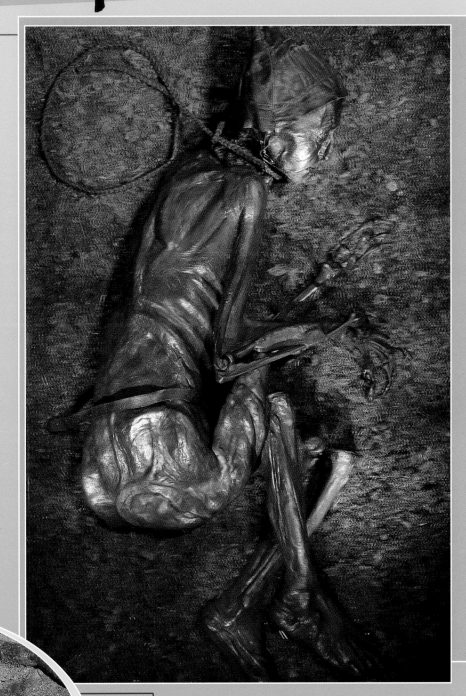

TEENS, TOO

In 1952, a 14-year-old female bog body was found in Windeby, Germany. Her blond hair was shaved off the left side of her head, and she was blindfolded with a colored cloth. Like other bog bodies, she was killed as a sacrifice. Large stones were used to pin Windeby Girl to the bottom of the bog, where she drowned, sometime during the first century A.D.

The Deep Freeze

S ome of the oldest and best-preserved mummies are formed accidentally by extreme cold—freezing temperatures prevent bacteria from causing decay. Sometimes ice mummies are preserved further by becoming freeze-dried. This happens when conditions are dry and windy as well as extremely cold. Scientists must store ice mummies in large walk-in freezers, from which they can be removed for only short periods. If exposed to warm temperatures for too long, bacteria and fungi will start to grow on the bodies, beginning the process of decomposition.

IT WASN'T A BON VOYAGE

More than 150 years ago, Sir John Franklin set sail from England to find a shortcut to the Pacific by following a path between Canada and the Arctic Circle. He was never heard from again—the expedition got trapped in ice after going in the wrong direction. A few years later, search parties discovered three graves on a tiny Arctic island. Inside the graves were the well-preserved ice mummies of three crew members, including John Torrington (right), who had died during the first year of the trip.

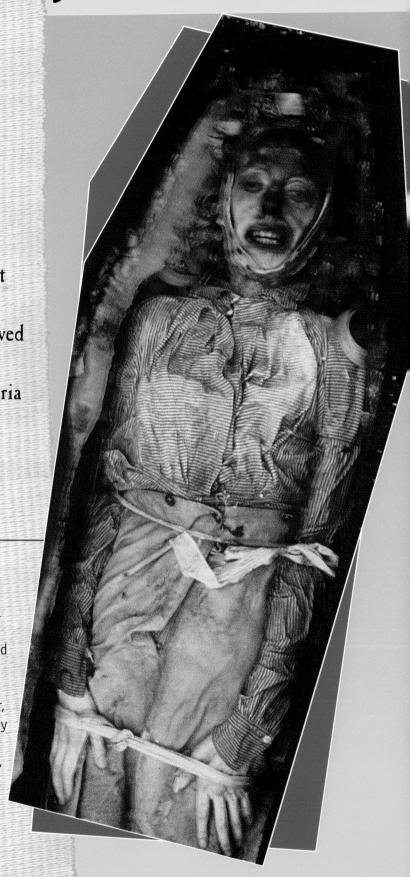

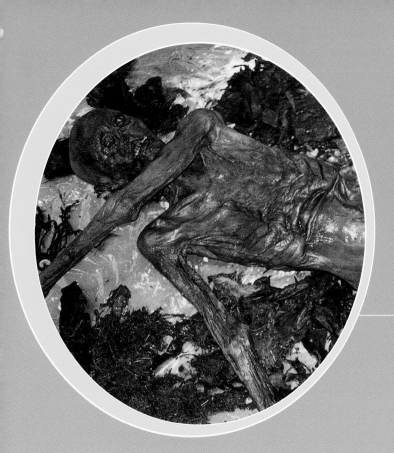

THE ICE MAN

Another famous frozen mummy is the Ice Man, who has the prestige of being the oldest well-preserved human mummy in the world. How old? About 5,300 years! In 1991, hikers found him frozen in a glacier in the Alps near the border of Italy and Austria. By studying his body, which was covered with tattoos, and his clothing and tools, scientists are trying to figure out who the Ice Man was and how he lived and died.

Forty-seven small marks on the Ice Man's body suggest that he had received acupuncture treatments for back pain—2,000 years before acupuncture was believed to be invented!

ESKIMO MUMMIES

Two brothers hunting on a jagged hillside in Qilakitsoq on the western coast of Greenland in 1972 made an amazing discovery. Two flat rocks that seemed out of place caught their attention. Beneath each one was a stone tomb about three feet deep. Inside were the freeze-dried mummies of eight Inuit women and children, whose ages ranged from 6 months to about 50 years. The bodies were stacked on top of each other, with five bodies in one grave and three in the other. They were all dressed in sealskin, to keep them warm on their journey to the Inuit Land of the Dead. Scientists believe they were buried in their rocky tomb around 1475.

ICY TOMB

In 1993, a group of Russian archaeologists in Siberia discovered the tomb of a woman of the ancient Pazyryk people, a tribe of warriors who lived more than 2,000 years ago. Buried more than seven feet under the frozen ground, the tomb was filled with ice because water had leaked into it and froze! The woman's body was inside a coffin carved from a single log. The decorative animal tattoos on her body, along with wooden figures of mythological animals and a stone bowl with ashes of burned herbs found with her, led the archaeologists to believe that she was a Pazyryk sorceress.

T he most common way that mummies are created, both accidentally by nature and intentionally by people, is by rapid drying. There are many ways in which a dead body may dry out. The climate may preserve a body if it is especially hot, dry, or both. Some mummies are created when exposed to moisture-absorbing substances, like salt. Other mummies are created by drying with hot smoke, just like beef jerky! Water is the number one enemy of dried mummies. If they get damp, even from just a small change in the moisture content of the air, bacteria will get to work and quickly start decomposition.

JUST HANGING OUT

In Papua New Guinea, people used to hang their dead relatives in the trees to dry in the hot sun. Then they further dried the bodies with smoke, covered them with a layer of clay, and propped them up on scaffolding to overlook the village.

DO-IT-YOURSELF MUMMIFICATION

From the late 1300s to the early 1900s, some Buddhist priests in Japan practiced a bizarre form of mummification—on themselves! While on a starvation diet, a priest waited for death surrounded by huge candles. By the time he finally died, his body would be practically mummified from the heat of the burning candles. The body would be kept in an underground tomb, but three years later the other priests would once again smoke-dry him with more candles, just to make sure the mummification was complete. Finally, the mummy would be set up in a temple where it could be worshipped like a statue.

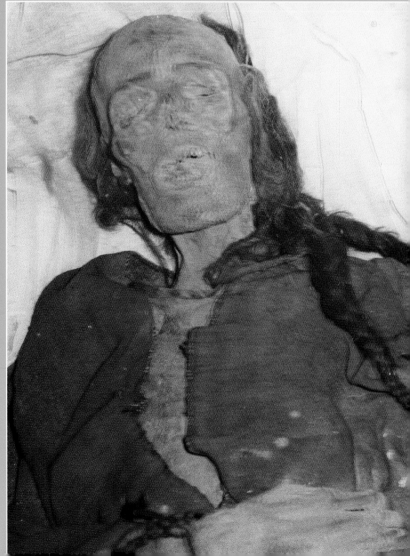

Place to Go

NOT EXACTLY THE SMITHSONIAN

The bodies buried in the cemetery in Guanajuato, Mexico, were naturally mummified by the dry sand and the hot climate. But we wouldn't have known this if it wasn't for a local law that was in effect from 1896 to 1958. Living relatives were required to pay a yearly fee to keep their loved ones buried. If they didn't pay the 20 pesos, the body would be dug up and put on display in El Museo de las Momias (The Museum of the Mummies). The law has been changed so that bodies are no longer dug up, but the museum is still in operation and open to tourists.

MYSTERIOUS MUMMIES OF CHINA

The hot, dry, and salty sand of western China's Taklimakan Desert is responsible for the creation of more than 100 wonderfully preserved mummies that are up to 4,000 years old. These mummies and the items found buried with them have archaeologists completely perplexed. The pattern on their clothing does not look like anything the ancient Chinese ever created. Even more peculiar, their hair is reddish blond, their eyes are round, and they have rather long noses. These Chinese mummies look far more European than Chinese! So where did these mystery mummies come from, and how did they end up in the Taklimakan Desert?

PRETTY WOMAN

Another well-preserved mummy of the Taklimakan Desert is affectionately named after the town near which she was discovered. The Beauty of Loulan was discovered in 1980 and died around 1800 B.C.

Modern Mummies

M ummies were created in ancient times as a way to cheat death. It was believed that if the body was still around, then the person must somehow still be living. But not all mummies were made thousands of years ago. Some mummies were created within the last century...and some are still being made today! And like their ancient counterparts, these modern mummies also cheat death—by sticking around, they serve as a constant reminder and live on in our memories.

WHEN NINE LIVES AREN'T ENOUGH

Unwilling to say good-bye to their pets, some people are choosing to have them professionally mummified instead! A company in Missouri freeze-dries pets in lifelike poses, while another in Utah combines modern technology with Egyptian tradition: each chemically mummified pet receives its own bronze coffin in the shape of the animal's own body!

MUMMIES MADE-TO-ORDER

A company in Salt Lake City specializes in mummifying humans by wrapping them in bandages, just like the ancient Egyptians. You can also order an Egyptian-style bronze sarcophagus— designed in the image of your favorite Pharaoh!

Have you heard the rumor that Walt Disney's head is frozen and buried in Disneyland? It's not true. Disney was cremated on December 17, 1966, and the ashes are at Forest Lawn Cemetery in California.

THE BIG CHILL

Faced with terminal illness, as many as forty people have chosen to have their bodies frozen in liquid nitrogen, hoping to be thawed some day in the future when the cure for their fatal disease is found. This practice, called cryonics, has been around since the 1960s. So why isn't everyone doing it? For starters, it's expensive. One company charges $135,000 to freeze the whole body (or $70,000 for the head only!), plus $300 a year for operating costs. Second, no one knows for sure if the body will be able to be revived after thawing, because when tissues freeze, ice crystals cause damage to the body's cells. But who knows, maybe in the future that won't be a problem!

MUMMY OF MOSCOW

The mummified body of Vladimir Lenin, the founder of the Soviet state, has been on display in the great mausoleum in Moscow's Red Square since his death in 1924. Lenin looks so good that some people insist the body must be a wax dummy. The process used to preserve his body remains a secret. It is rumored that Pedro Ara, the man who mummified Evita Perón, the immensely popular wife of Argentine president Juan Perón, was involved. But since Ara is long dead, we'll never know for sure.

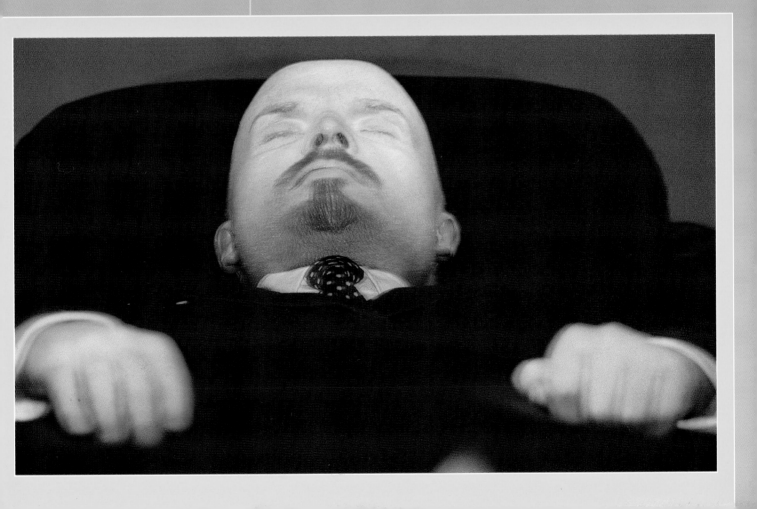

Bolivian Cochabamba pre-Columbian mummies in baskets dated A.D. 500–1000.

Copyright © 2000 by Arcturus Publishing Limited
1-7 Shand Street, London SE1 2ES England
All rights reserved.

Discovery Communications, Inc.
John S. Hendricks, *Founder, Chairman, and Chief Executive Officer*
Judith A. McHale, *President and Chief Operating Officer*
Judy L. Harris, *Senior Vice President and General Manager, Consumer Products*
Marjorie Kaplan, *Senior Vice President, Children's Programming and Products*

Discovery Publishing
Natalie Chapman, *Vice President, Publishing*
Rita Thievon Mullin, *Editorial Director*
Tracy Fortini, *Product Development, Discovery Channel Retail*

Discovery Kids™, which includes Saturday and Sunday morning programming on Discovery Channel®, Discoverykids.com, and the digital showcase network, is dedicated to encouraging and empowering kids to explore the world around them.

Discovery Channel® and Discovery Kids™ are trademarks of Discovery Communications, Inc.

Published in the United States 2001 by Dutton Children's Books, a division of Penguin Putnam Books for Young Readers
345 Hudson Street, New York, New York 10014
www.penguinputnam.com

Author: Kevin Fleury
Editor: Meredith Mundy Wasinger
Consulting Editor: Jennifer Houser Wegner
Designers: Dan Hosek and Susi Martin

Picture Credits:
AKG/Erich Lessing: title page; page 15, bottom.
Ancient Art & Architecture: page 7, top right.
The Ancient Egypt Picture Library: front cover; page 3, bottom left; page 4, top center.
The Art Archive: back cover; page 2, left.
CM Dixon: page 8, top center.
Eurelios/Phillippe Plailly: page 5, bottom; page 7, bottom left.
Robert Harding Picture Library: page 8; page 9, bottom left.
Rex Features: page 2, center; page 3, right; page 11, top left.
Science Photo Library: page 9, right.
South American Picture Library: page 6, center; page 13, left; page 16.
Frank Spooner Picture Library: page 5, top; page 12, right; page 15, top.
Sygma: page 4, bottom; page 13, right; page 14.
Topham Picturepoint: page 10, right.
Werner Forman Archive: page 11, bottom right.

3-D images produced by Pinsharp

Printed in China   First Edition
ISBN: 0-525-46470-0